Tree or Three?

Tree or Three?

An elementary pronunciation course

Ann Baker

with drawings by Leslie Marshall

CAMBRIDGE
UNIVERSITY PRESS

PUBLISHED BY THE PRESS SYNDICATE OF THE UNIVERSITY OF CAMBRIDGE
The Pitt Building, Trumpington Street, Cambridge, United Kingdom

CAMBRIDGE UNIVERSITY PRESS
The Edinburgh Building, Cambridge CB2 2RU, UK   www.cup.cam.ac.uk
40 West 20th Street, New York, NY 10011-4211, USA   www.cup.org
10 Stamford Road, Oakleigh, Melbourne 3166, Australia
Ruiz de Alarcón 13, 28014 Madrid, Spain

First published 1982
Eighteenth printing 1999

Printed in the United Kingdom at the University Press, Cambridge

ISBN 0 521 28293 4 *Tree or three?* Student's Book
ISBN 0 521 28580 1 *Introducing English Pronunciation*, A Teacher's Guide
ISBN 0 521 26355 7 Cassette Set

Contents

To the student

About this book

It is for beginner and elementary students of English as a Foreign Language.

What the book does

It teaches you to pronounce English correctly. This is important if you want to talk to people in English and be understood by them. It also helps you to understand people when they talk to you.

How to use the book

You will need to look at the book and listen carefully to the instructions on the cassettes. Sometimes you have to repeat what you hear; sometimes you have to ask or answer questions. Almost all the exercises are recorded on the cassettes and many of the activities you can do with a friend.

 means the exercise is on the cassette.

means the answer is on pages 120 and 121 of the book.

To the teacher

This is a pronunciation course for beginners and elementary students in English as a Foreign Language. Structures and, with very few exceptions, vocabulary are those familiar to most students at this level. So that beginners can have the advantage of a structurally graded course and at the same time practice material relevant to their needs, the sounds taught at the beginning of the book include those that nearly all students have difficulty with. The accompanying teacher's book provides notes on linking up this material with general structure teaching and spelling, information on pronunciation difficulties of different national groups, and suggestions for lesson procedures and further practice.

The course has been developed for use in the classroom as well as for students working alone. All exercises with this symbol [⚏] are recorded on cassette together with additional practice material. The key symbol ⚎ following an exercise indicates that the answers are given at the back of the book.

Unit 1

S

sun

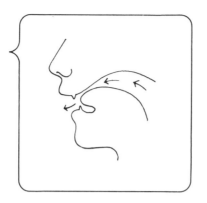

Exercise 1

Listen and repeat:

1 a bus

2 a glass

3 a horse

4 a house

5 a **bi**cycle

6 a po**lice**man

7 a **pen**cil

8 a box

9 a star

10 a stick

11 a spoon

12 a desk

3

Sentence practice

EXAMPLE: Picture 1

Student A: **What's this**?
Student B: It's a **bus**.

Exercise 2

Dialogue:

Miss Smith: **What's this, Sam**?
Sam: It's a **bicycle**.
Miss Smith: And **what's this**?
Sam: It's a **house**.
Miss Smith: **What's this**? A **bus**?
Sam: **Yes**.
Miss Smith: And **what's this**? A **horse**?
Sam: **No**, Miss **Smith**. It's a **police**man!

Exercise 3

Sentence practice

EXAMPLE: cup

Answer: It's a **cup**.   They're **cups**.

1 ship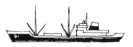

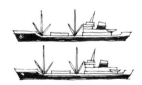

4

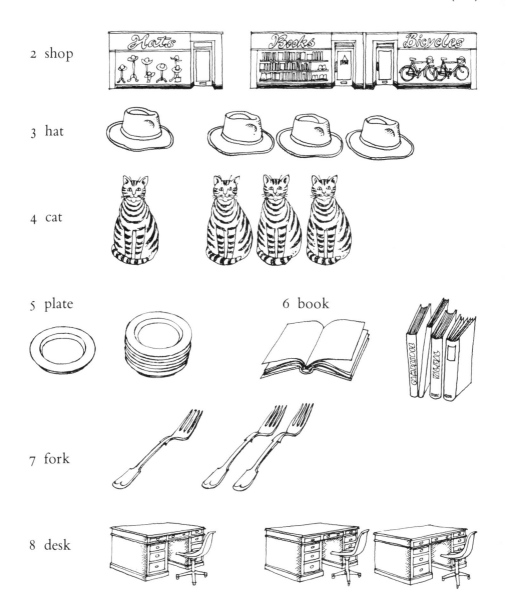

2 shop

3 hat

4 cat

5 plate

6 book

7 fork

8 desk

Exercise 4 🖭

Listen and repeat:

pencil	**pic**ture	**bi**cycle	po**lice**man
answer	**u**nit	**di**alogue	exam**ple**
listen	**stu**dent	**e**xercise	

Unit 2

z

zoo

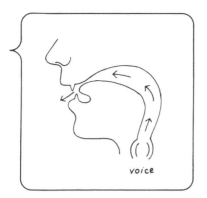

voice

Exercise 1

Listen and repeat:

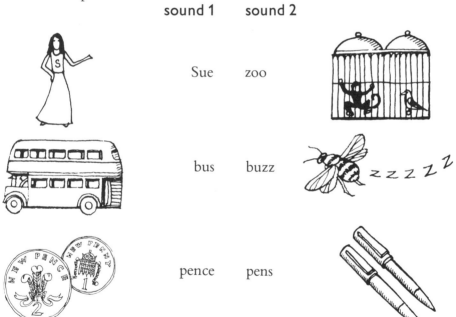

	sound 1	sound 2	
	Sue	zoo	
	bus	buzz	
	pence	pens	

Look at the pairs of sentences below. Put a tick against the sentences you hear.

a) Look at that Sue!   Look at that zoo!

b) Listen to that bus!   Listen to that buzz!

c) Ten pence, please.   Ten pens, please.

6

Exercise 2

Listen and repeat:

Is **this** a **box**?

No, it **isn't**.

It's a **house**.

Sentence practice

1 horse	2 hat	3 star	4 cup	5 book	6 spoon

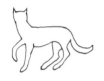   

| cat | plate | the sun | glass | box | |

EXAMPLE: Picture 1

Student A: Is **this** a **horse**?

Student B: **No**, it **isn't**. It's a **cat**.

Exercise 3

Sentence practice

EXAMPLE: Picture 1

These are **flow**ers and **those** are **trees**.

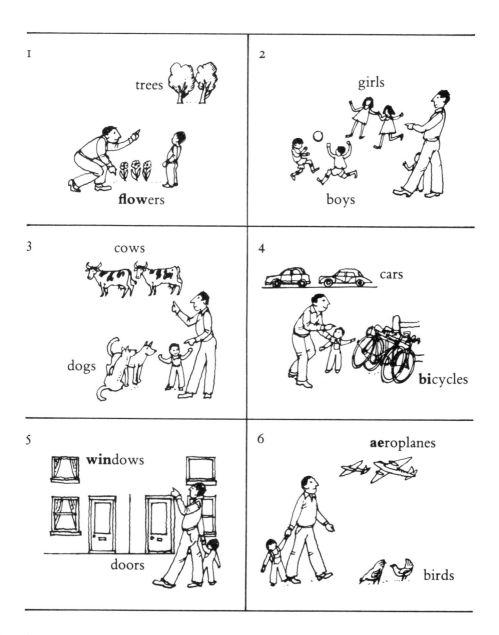

Exercise 4 📼

Listen and repeat:

question	**e**xercise	po**lice**man
answer	**di**alogue	ex**am**ple
window	**ae**roplane	
isn't	**bi**cycle	
flower		

Unit 3

ə

a camera

ə camərə

In this unit the spelling shows the sound ə.

Exercise 1

Listen and repeat:

questiən   **ex**əcise   pə**lice**mən
answə   **di**əlogue
flowə   **aer**əplane

Sentence practice

EXAMPLE: Picture 1

It's ə pə**lice**mən.

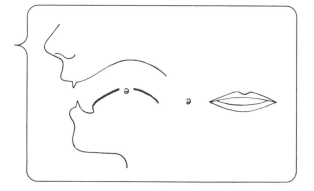

1   ə pə**lice**mən   .2   ə **flow**ə

Is that
ə flowə?

Yes, it is.

3   ən **aer**əplane   4   ə **ques**tıən   5   ən **an**swə

10

Exercise 2

EXAMPLE:    plates

Student A: **ə these plates?**
Student B: **No, they aren't.**

1	2	3

doors   **pen**cils   spoons

4	5	6

aerəplanes   trees   **bi**cycles

7	8

shops   hats

11

Unit 4

θ

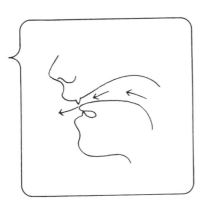

thin

Exercise 1

Listen and repeat:

	sound 1	sound 2	
	mouse	mouth	
	sum	thumb	
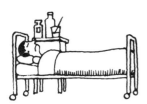	sick	thick	

Look at the pairs of sentences below. Put a tick against the sentences you hear.

a) Is that a mouse?   Is that a mouth?

b) Look at this sum.   Look at this thumb.

c) It's sick.   It's thick.

Exercise 2

Listen and repeat:

1st	first	6th	sixth
2nd	**se**cond	7th	**se**venth
3rd	third	8th	eighth
4th	fourth	9th	ninth
5th	fifth	10th	tenth

Sentence practice

Look at the picture.

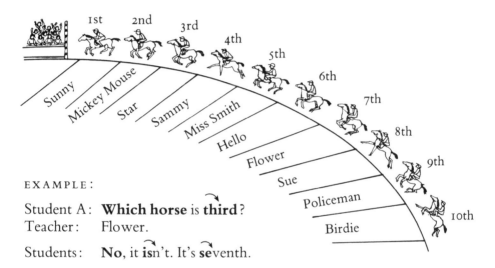

EXAMPLE:

Student A: **Which horse** is **third**?

Teacher: Flower.

Students: **No**, it **isn't**. It's **se**venth.

Unit 5

ð

feather

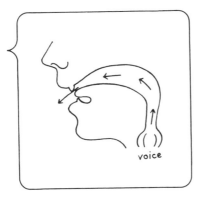

voice

Exercise 1

Listen and repeat:

This is   This is

                 This is   This is

a man   a **wo**man   a boy   a girl

Now listen.
There are two boys here:

Which boy is in the first picture?
The boy with the book or the boy
with the bicycle?

The boy with the book.

Sentence practice

EXAMPLE:

Student A: **Which boy** is in the **first pic**ture?

Student B: The **boy** with the **book**.

14

3   4   5   6

7   8

Exercise 2 🔲

Listen and repeat:
mother   **grand**mother
father   **grand**father
brother

Sentence practice 🔲

This is Sue with a
picture of her family.
Answer the questions
below.

Which one is Sue's │ mother?
│ father?
│ brother?
│ grandmother?
│ grandfather?
Which one is Sue?

Unit 6

iː

sheep

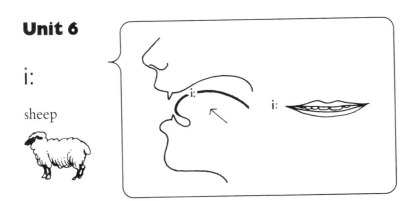

Exercise 1

sandwiches   MENU   drinks

meat   cheese   tea   coffee

Listen and repeat:

A **cheese sand**wich, please, and a **cup** of **tea**.

A **meat sand**wich, please, and **tea**.

A **cup** of **tea** for **me**, please.

Two cheese sandwiches, **one meat** sandwich, and **three teas**, please.

2 **cheese**. . 1 **meat**. . . . 3 **teas**.

Practise from the menu:

Exercise 2

Numbers and Letters:

Say these numbers:
three   thir**teen**   3   13   4   14   5   15   6   16   7   17   8   18   9   19

Say these letters: b   c   d   e   g   p   t   v

Spell these words: cup   thirteen   book   sheep   tea
                    plate   seventeen   desk   cheese   meat
                    sandwich   eighteen   stick coffee   please

Unit 7

ɪ

ship

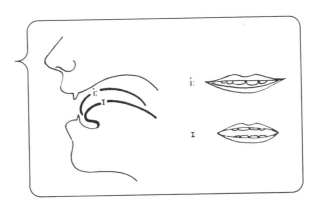

Exercise 1

Listen and repeat:

	sound 1	sound 2	
	sheep	ship	
	bean	bin	
	meal	mill	

Look at the pairs of sentences below. Put a tick against the sentences you hear.

a) Look at the sheep.   Look at the ship.
b) These are beans.   These are bins.
c) Is this a meal?   Is this a mill?

18

Exercise 2

Sentence practice

EXAMPLE: Picture 1

It's a **little sheep**.

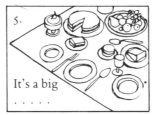

| 1. It's a little . . . . . | 2. It's a big . . . . . | 3. It's a big . . . . . |
| 4. It's a little . . . . . | 5. It's a big . . . . . | 6. It's a little . . . . . |

What's this? It's a **little ba**by.

Here are eight babies:

1

2

3

4

5

6

7

8

Listen and repeat:
big **little heavy hungry happy thirsty funny dirty**

Sentence practice

EXAMPLE: Picture 1

It's a **little ba**by.

19

Exercise 3

Listen and repeat:

3	three	13	thir**teen**	30	**thir**ty
4	four	14	four**teen**	40	**for**ty
5	five	15	fif**teen**	50	**fif**ty
6	six	16	six**teen**	60	**six**ty
7	**se**ven	17	seven**teen**	70	**se**venty
8	eight	18	eigh**teen**	80	**eigh**ty
9	nine	19	nine**teen**	90	**nine**ty

Exercise 4

Listen and repeat:

horses	**bo**xes	**sand**wiches
faces	**si**xes	
glasses	**no**ses	
buses	**hou**ses	

Sentence practice

EXAMPLE:

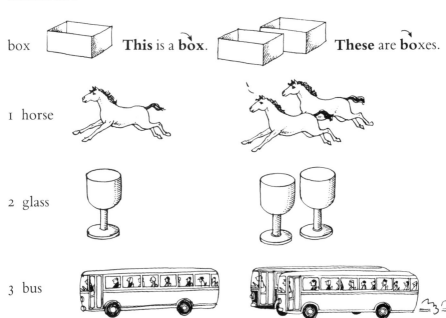

box   **This** is a **bóx**.   **These** are **bó**xes.

1 horse

2 glass

3 bus

20

4 six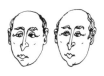

5 face

6 nose

7 house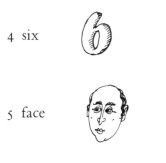

8 sandwich

Unit 8

f

fan

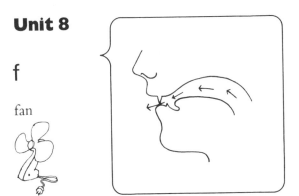

Four Friends 📼

Listen and repeat:

four fish

some flowers

a telephone

a fly

a fork

a fire

some fruit

a knife

a leaf

Fred and Fay

the floor

Finish these sentences:
1 .... is fat.
2 Fay's hat .... funny.
3 There's a .... on the floor.
4 There's a .... on Fred's head.
5 The four .... are in front of the fire.

22

Unit 9

V

van

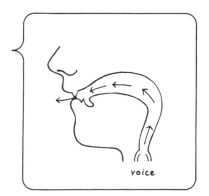

voice

Exercise 1 📼

Victor

Vera

Fred

Fay

Fred and Fay are visitors.
They are visiting Victor and Vera.
What have Victor and Vera got?   They've got a telephone.
                                   They've got some flowers.

Now you try: They've got ....

Sentence practice 📼

EXAMPLE: Student A: Have they **got** ★a **te**levision?
            Student B: **No**, they **ha**ven't.

★Substitute:
  a **bowl** of **fruit**   **twelve forks**   a **very big fish**
  a **vase** of **flow**ers   **eleven flow**ers   **two** very **funny friends**
  five fish   **seven flies**

23

Unit 10

W

window

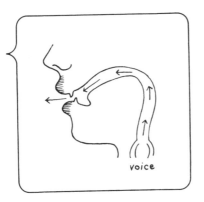

voice

Exercise 1

Listen and repeat:

	sound 1	sound 2	
	vet	wet	
	vine	wine	
	veil	whale	

Look at the pairs of sentences below. Put a tick against the sentences you hear.

a) He's a vet student.   He's a wet student.

b) There's a little vine here.   There's a little wine here.

c) That's a veil.   That's a whale.

Exercise 2

Listen and repeat:

What's the we͡ather like?

It's **warm**.   It's **wet**.   It's **win**dy.

Sentence practice

EXAMPLE:

Student A: **What's** the **wea**ther like in ....?

Student B:	It's It's **not**	**ve**ry	**wet** **warm** **win**dy

Exercise 3

Listen and repeat:

What's this?   It's a **watch**.

What's the **watch** like?   It's **square**.

   It's **quiet**.

What's the **time**?

It's **quar**ter past **twelve**.

It's **twen**ty past **twelve**.

Sentence practice

EXAMPLE:

Student A: What's the time?
Student B: It's quarter past one.

1   2   3   4   5

6   7   8

26

Unit 11

ə

a camera

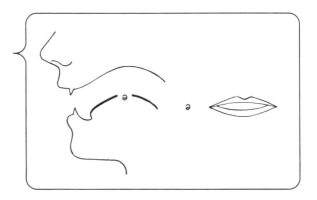

In this unit the spelling shows the sound ə.

Exercise 1

What's this?

1

It's ə **cup**
əf **co**ffee.

2

....
....

3

It's ə **vase**
əf **leaves**.

4

....
....

5

It's ə **bowl**
əf **fruit**.

6

....
....

7

It's ə **plate**
əf **cakes**.

8

....
....

Exercise 2

EXAMPLE:

Student A: Həve you got thə **time**?

Student B: Yes. It's eleven ə'clock.

I	2	3	4	5

6	7	8

Exercise 3

Ask and answer questions.

EXAMPLE:

I

Student A: Have you **got** ə teləphone?

Student B: **Yes**, I have. / **No**, I havən't.

2	3	4	5	6

28

7 8  9  10  11

12  13  14 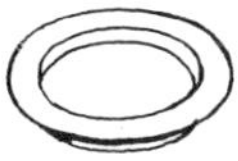 15  16

Unit 12

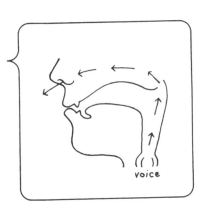

m

mouth

Exercise 1

Listen and repeat:

market

Come to the **mar**ket.

swimming pool

Come to the **swi**mming pool.

farm

Come to the **farm**.

home

Come home.

Sentence practice

EXAMPLE: Picture I

Come to the **mar**ket with **me**.

30

Unit 13

n

nose

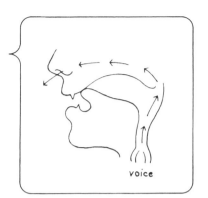

voice

Exercise 1

Listen and repeat:

	sound 1	sound 2	
	mice	nice	
	Tim	tin	
	Mummy	money	

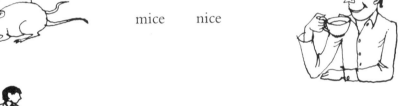

a) These are mice.   These are nice.
b) That's my little Tim.   That's my little tin.
c) That's her Mummy.   That's her money.

Exercise 2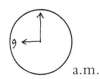

Numbers and Times

Listen and repeat:

1   9   10   15   16   18   19   21   29

a.m.   **nine** o'clock in the **mor**ning

one o'clock in the after**noon**

p.m.

ten o'clock in the **ev**ening

p.m.

What's the **time**?

1   a.m.   2   p.m.   3   a.m.   4   p.m.

7   **le**sson **se**ven
11 **Listen** to **le**sson e**leven**.
17 seven**teen stu**dents
70 **Se**ven **stu**dents **listen** to **le**sson **se**venty.
    Is **this le**sson **se**venty? **No**, it **isn't**!

Exercise 3

Dialogue:

A: **Come** to ★.................. with **me** to**morr**ow.

B: **What time**?

A: | **Nine**
| **One**
| **Se**ven | o'**clock**.
| **El**even |

B: In the **mor**ning?

A: **No**. In the | **eve**ning |
| after**noon** |.

★Substitute:

the **ci**nema   the **town**   the **moun**tains   the **moon**

33

Unit 14

ŋ

ring

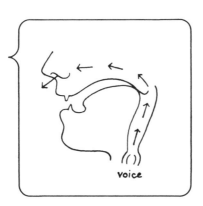

Exercise 1

Listen and repeat:

sound 1   sound 2

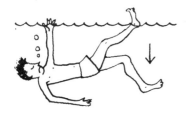

sink   sing

sinking   singing

Look at the pairs of sentences below. Put a tick against the sentences you hear.

a) Please don't sink!   Please don't sing!

b) Are you sinking?   Are you singing?

Exercise 2

Listen and repeat:

singing	**rea**ding a **book**	**wa**tching **te**levision
talking	**smo**king a **pipe**	**play**ing **ta**ble tennis
cooking	**wa**shing her **hair**	**li**stening to the **ra**dio
sleeping	**ea**ting an **apple**	
drinking **tea**		

34

Exercise 3

Sentence practice

EXAMPLES:

1 **Mr Long** is **slee**ping.

2 Student A: **What's Ben** doing?

  Student B: He's **rea**ding a **book** and **ea**ting an **a**pple.

Exercise 4 🖭

Dialogue

(**Mrs Long** is talking on the telephone.)

Mrs Young: Good morning, Mrs **Long**. How are you?

Mrs Long: I'm fine, **thanks**.

Mrs Young: **What** are you doing?

Mrs Long: I'm cooking.

Mrs Young: **What** are the children doing?

Mrs Long: **Ben** is reading. **Anne** is washing her **hair**. **Ron** and **Dan**
            are **play**ing table tennis.

Mrs Young: And **is** your **hus**band **wa**shing the **car** this morning?

Mrs Long: **No**, he isn't! He's sleeping!

Unit 15

e

pen

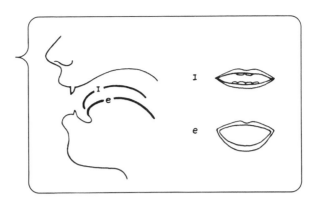

Exercise 1

Listen and repeat:

sound 1   sound 2

pin   pen

bin   Ben

tin   ten

Look at the pairs of sentences below. Put a tick against the sentences you hear.
a) Have you got a pin?   Have you got a pen?
b) That's my bin.   That's my Ben.
c) That tin is very small. That ten is very small.

37

Exercise 2

Listen and repeat:

Ben	**Betty**	**cl**ever	**better**
Fred	**Jenny**	**very cl**ever	best

Ben, Jenny, Betty and **Fred** are **very cl**ever.

Ben is a **very**   **Jenny** is **better**   **Betty** is **better**   **Fred** is the **best**
good student.   than **Ben**.   than **Jenny**.   **stu**dent.

Now look at the pictures again and ask and answer questions.

EXAMPLES:

1 Fred .... Ben
   Student A: Is **Fred better** than **Ben**?

   Student B: **Yes**.

2 Ben .... Betty
   Student A: Is **Ben better** than **Betty**?

   Student B: **No**. **Betty** is **better** than **Ben**.

1 Fred .... Ben	4 Betty .... Ben	7 Betty .... Fred
2 Ben .... Betty	5 Jenny .... Ben	8 Jenny .... Fred
3 Fred .... Jenny	6 Ben .... Jenny	9 Betty .... Jenny

Exercise 3

Say these letters: f   s   x   l   m   n
Spell these words:

left	**lesson**	**bo**xes
next	**listen**	**si**xes
men	**many**	second
thief	**money**	**funny**

Unit 16

æ

man

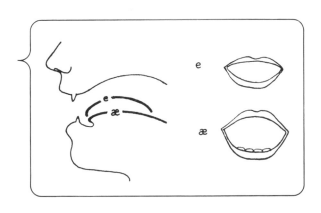

Exercise 1

Listen and repeat:

	sound 1	sound 2	
N	N	Anne	
X	X	axe	
	pen	pan	

Look at the pairs of sentences below. Put a tick against the sentences you hear.

a) Her name is Miss N. Smith.   Her name is Miss Anne Smith.
b) That's a very big X.   That's a very big axe.
c) Have you got a pen?   Have you got a pan?

Exercise 2

The Black Family

Grandmother
Black

Grandfather
Black

Janet
Black

Jack
Black.

Anne
Black

Patrick
Black

Listen and repeat:

Anne Black	**Janet Black**	**Grand**father **Black**
Jack Black	**Patrick Black**	**Grand**mother **Black**

Jack Black is **ve**ry **sad**.
Janet **Black** is **ve**ry **ha**ppy.
Grandmother **Black** is **ve**ry **fat**.
Anne Black is **ca**rrying a **bag**.
Grandfather **Black** is **wea**ring a **hat**.
Patrick **Black** is **loo**king at the **cat**.

Sentence practice

EXAMPLE:

Student A: **Grand**mother **Black** is **ve**ry **fat**.
Student B: They're **all ve**ry **fat** ex**cept** for **Jack**.

Unit 17

ʌ

cup

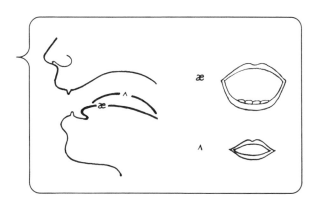

Exercise 1

Listen and repeat:

	sound 1	sound 2
	cap	cup
	hat	hut
	cat	cut

Look at the pairs of sentences below. Put a tick against the sentences you hear.
a) Is this your cap?   Is this your cup?
b) Look at that little hat.   Look at that little hut.
c) That's a very bad cat.   That's a very bad cut.

Exercise 2

Listen and repeat:
Boys' names: Sam Dan Jack **An**drew **Pat**rick
Girls' names: Anne Pam **Jan**et **Pat**sy **Sal**ly
Surnames: Love Young **Lon**don **Mon**day

A Family Tree:

THE YOUNG FAMILY

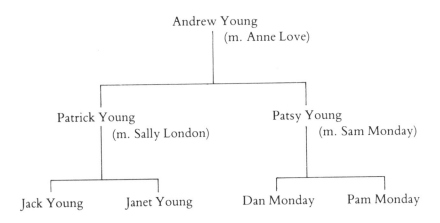

Listen and repeat:
son **mo**ther **bro**ther **hus**band **un**cle **cou**sin **grand**son
grandmother

Now look at the family tree and choose the correct word to finish these
sentences:

1 **Pat**sy **Young** is **Dan Mon**day's .... **grand**mother/**mo**ther.
2 **Sam Mon**day is **Pat**sy **Young**'s .... **hus**band/**bro**ther.
3 **Dan Mon**day is **Sam Mon**day's .... son/**bro**ther.
4 **Dan Mon**day is **Pam Mon**day's .... **un**cle/**bro**ther.
5 **Anne Love** is **Dan Mon**day's .... **mo**ther/**grand**mother.
6 **Dan Mon**day is **An**drew **Young**'s .... **grand**son/son.
7 **Pat**rick **Young** is **Dan Mon**day's .... **bro**ther/**un**cle.
8 **Jack** and **Jan**et **Young** are **Dan's** .... **un**cles/**cou**sins.
9 **Sal**ly **Lon**don has **just one** .... son/**grand**son.
10 **Jan**et **Young** has **just one** .... **bro**ther/**cou**sin.

Unit 18

ɑ:

heart

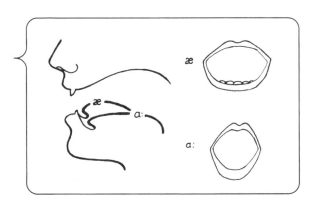

Exercise 1

Listen and repeat:

sound 1   sound 2

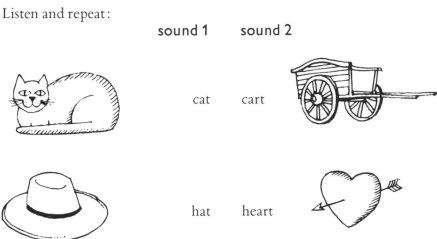

	sound 1	sound 2	
	cat	cart	
	hat	heart	

Look at the pairs of sentences below. Put a tick against the sentences you hear.

a) I've got a little cat.   I've got a little cart.

b) That's a lovely hat.   That's a lovely heart.

43

Listen and repeat:

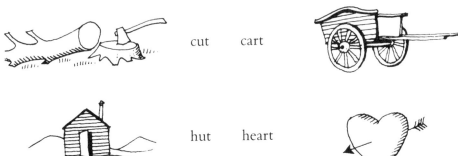

sound 1   sound 2

cut   cart

hut   heart

Look at the pairs of sentences below. Put a tick against the sentences you hear.
a) That's a very bad cut.   That's a very bad cart.
b) Look at that hut.   Look at that heart.

Exercise 2

Listen and repeat:

Can you **hear** me, **Grand**father?

Can you **see** me, **Grand**father?

Yes, I **can**.

No, I **can't**.

bananas
tomatoes   **gla**sses

plants

grass

Uncle **Charles**   **Aunt Ann**   **Grand**father

Grandfather is in the **gar**den.
Are **Charles** and **Ann** as**king ques**tions?   **Yes**, they **are**.
Are they **an**swering **ques**tions?   **No**, they **aren't**.

44

Practise these questions and answers:

Student A: Are the
bananas	on the **grass**
tomatoes	on the **table**
glasses	in the **gar**den
plants	
?

Student B:
| **Yes**, they **are** |
| **No**, they **aren't** |
.

Unit 19

h

hat

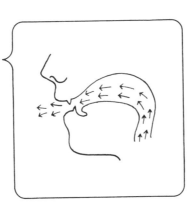

Exercise 1

Listen and repeat:

sound 1 (no sound)	sound 2
E	he
is	his
I	high
ill	hill

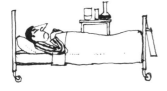

Exercise 2

Listen and repeat:

1

a horse
an **e**lephant

2

an **ae**roplane
a hand bag

3

a hat
a house

4

an egg
an **a**pple

Sentence practice

EXAMPLES:

Student A: **Whose horse** is **this**?
Student B: It's **his**.

Student A: **Whose e**lephant is **this**?
Student B: It's **hers**.

Exercise 3 🖭

Dialogue:

A: Hello.
B: Hello. How are you?
A: I'm fine, thanks. How are you?
B: All right. How's your *father?
A: He's very well, thanks.

*Substitute:
brother   uncle   grandfather

Exercise 4 🖭

Reading

An old man is very ill and he goes into hospital to have an operation.
He is very unhappy and afraid.
When he arrives at the hospital a nurse gives him a bath.
After the bath he is very happy and he says to the nurse, 'I was very
afraid to have that operation but it didn't hurt me at all.'

Unit 20

ɒ

clock

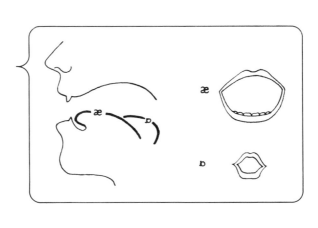

Exercise 1

Listen and repeat:

sound 1   sound 2

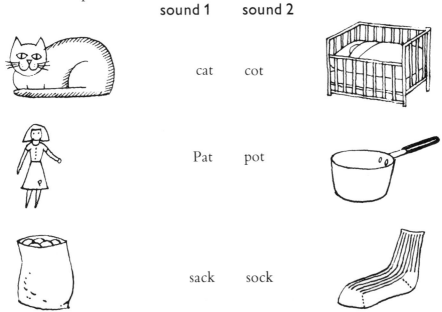

	sound 1	sound 2
	cat	cot
	Pat	pot
	sack	sock

Look at the pairs of sentences below. Put a tick against the sentences you hear.

a) I want a white cat, please.   I want a white cot, please.

b) That Pat is very strong.   That pot is very strong.

c) There's a sack on the floor.   There's a sock on the floor.

49

Listen and repeat:

sound 1	sound 2	sound 3	sound 4
hat	hut	heart	hot
cat	cut	cart	cot

Exercise 2

Sentence practice

EXAMPLE:

Student A: **What** have they **got** in the **first shop**?

Student B: A **lot** of **clocks**.

Exercise 3 🔲

Dialogue:

Customer: Have you **got** any ★**pots**?

Shop Assistant: **Yes**. We've **got** a **lot** of **pots**.

Customer: I **want** a **very strong pot, please.**

★Substitute:
clocks	**hand**bags
sacks	**wa**tches
cots	**bo**xes

Unit 21

ɔː

ball

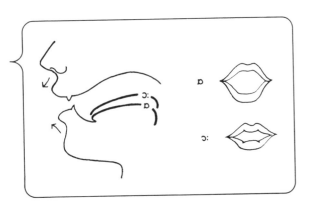

Exercise 1 🔊

Listen and repeat:

sound 1   sound 2

Don   Dawn

pot   port

fox   forks

Look at the pairs of sentences below. Put a tick against the sentences you hear.
a) Is your name Don? Is your name Dawn?
b) That's a very big pot. That's a very big port.
c) We don't want the fox in here. We don't want the forks in here.

Exercise 2

Listen and repeat:

It's a **large ball**.   It's a **small ball**.

It's a **long fork**.

It's a **short fork**.

He's a **tall foot**baller.   He's a **short foot**baller.

Describe these:

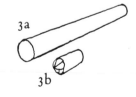

1a 1b

2a 2b

3a

3b

doctors   **bo**xes   **pie**ces of **chalk**

Exercise 3

Which picture shows:
a **shop** with **four tall doc**tors in it.
a **hut** with **four small fo**xes in it.
a **long wall** with a **small door** in it.
a **bath** with a **lot** of **hot wa**ter in it.

Now you try drawing:
a long box with a lot of small balls in it.
a large house with four small windows and a door
a tall glass with a little water in it

Unit 22

 ə a camera

In this unit the spelling shows where to make the sound ə.

Exercise 1

Listen and repeat:

mothə   **sis**tə   **fa**thə

grandmothə   **bro**thə   **grand**fathə

Sentence practice

EXAMPLES:

Is **that** your **mo**thə?   Is **that** your **mo**thər ənd **fa**thə?

1   2   3   4   5

6   7   8   9   10

55

Exercise 2

Look again at the picture in Unit 18 Exercise 2.

EXAMPLE:

Aunt Ann: Cən you **hear**?

Grandfathə: **Yes,** I **can**.

hear

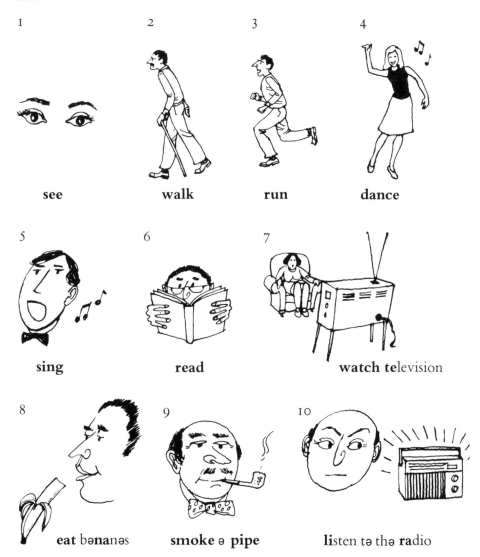

1

see

2

walk

3

run

4

dance

5

sing

6

read

7

watch television

8

eat bənanəs

9

smoke ə **pipe**

10

listen tə thə **ra**dio

Riddles⋆

1 **What is** it?   **I** cən **see** it bət **you can't**.
2 **What is** it?   **You** cən **see** it bət **I can't**.

⋆ Riddles are question and answer jokes. Answers: 1. The back of your head. 2. The back of my head.

Unit 23

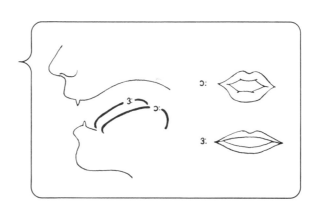

ɜː

girl

Exercise 1

Listen and repeat:

	sound 1	sound 2	
	Paul	Pearl	
	shorts	shirts	
	walks	works	

Look at the pairs of sentences below. Put a tick against the sentences you hear.

a) Is your name Paul?   Is your name Pearl?
b) I want white shorts, please.   I want white shirts, please.
c) He walks in the garden.   He works in the garden.

58

Exercise 2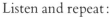

Listen and repeat:

a **bird**

a **worm**

It's **ear**ly in the **mor**ning

a **bird** in a **warm nest**

Learn this proverb:

'IT'S THE **EAR**LY **BIRD** THAT **CA**TCHES THE **WORM**'

Exercise 3

Listen and repeat:

1 **Pearl** is a **wor**king **girl**. She **gets up** **ear**ly.

2 **Pearl's thir**sty in the **mor**ning.

3 She **puts on** a **short shirt** and a **long skirt**.

It's the **ear**ly **bird** that **ca**tches the **worm**!

4 She **walks** to **work** at **se**ven **thir**ty.

5 Pearl a**rri**ves at **work** at **eight** **thir**ty.

6 She's the **first** **per**son at **work**.

59

Unit 24

A

l

letter

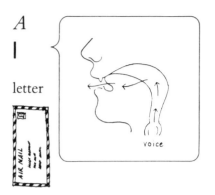

B

l

ball

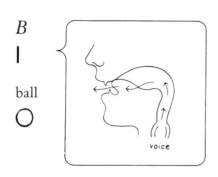

O

Sound A

Exercise 1

Listen and repeat:

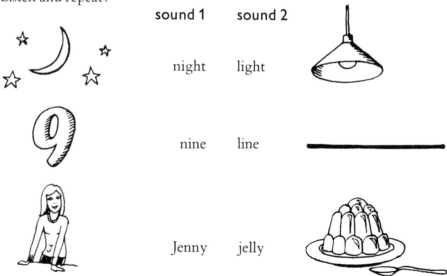

	sound 1	sound 2	
	night	light	
	nine	line	
	Jenny	jelly	

Look at the pairs of sentences below. Put a tick against the sentences you hear.
a) It's a lovely night.   It's a lovely light.
b) Draw a nine.   Draw a line.
c) He loves Jenny.   He loves jelly.

60

Exercise 2

Listen and repeat:

i.

a **le**mon **je**lly   a **ye**llow **te**lephone   a **co**lour **te**levision

ii)

a **black plate**

a **clean glass**

a **blue flow**er

a **love**ly **plant**

a **slow ae**roplane   a **cle**ver **class**

Sound B

Exercise 1

Listen and repeat:

| | sound 1 | sound 2 |

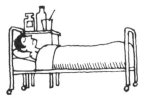

| | bin | Bill |

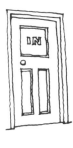

| | in | ill |

| | pin | pill |

Look at the pairs of sentences below. Put a tick against the sentences you hear.

a) That's my bin.   That's my Bill.
b) He's in. He's ill.
c) He wants a pin. He wants a pill.

Exercise 2

Listen and repeat:

i)

a **ball**   a **school**girl   a **small hill**   a **full** hotel

ii)

an old man

cold milk

twelve children

iii)

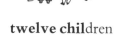

an **a**pple

a **pu**pil

people

an ex**am**ple

a **bo**ttle

a **ta**ble

a **pen**cil

a **bi**cycle

a **li**ttle **a**nimal

Sounds A and B

Exercise 3 🔲

EXAMPLES:

A: **That** hotel is **full**.

B: **Those** hotels are **all full**.

A: **This** table is **clean**.

B: **These** tables are **all clean**.

1 **This meal** is **cold**.
2 **This ball** is **little**.
3 **That girl** is **clever**.
4 **That hill** is **small**.
5 **This school** is **cold**.
6 **This wall** is **old**.

7 **That bicycle** is **slow**.
8 **This animal** is **clever**.
9 **This table** is **clean**.
10 **That pupil** is **sleeping**.
11 **This example** is **difficult**.
12 **That pencil** is **black**.

Unit 25

r

rain

voice

Exercise 1

A

Listen and repeat:

	sound 1	sound 2	

$$10 + 7 + 2 + 3$$
$$+ 9 + 1 + 4$$
$$+ 5 = 41$$

long   wrong

$$4 + 4 = 9$$

jelly   Jerry

glass   grass

Look at the pairs of sentences below. Put a tick against the sentences you hear.

a) It's a long sum.   It's a wrong sum.
b) Mary likes jelly.   Mary likes Jerry.
c) There's a flower in the glass.   There's a flower in the grass.

65

Exercise 2

Ron   Mary   Jenny

Ron, **Mary** and **Jenny** are **all go**ing a**long** the **road.**

Who's | **ru**nning
riding a **bi**cycle | a**long** the **road**?
carrying a **te**levision

Jenny, **Fred** and **Patrick** are **all**
going a**long** the **street.**

Sentence practice 🔲

EXAMPLE:

Student A: **Who's** *⌐**thro**wing a b͡all **along** the street?
Student B: **Fr͡ed** is.

*Substitute:
 dropping **fruit** **wa**tering **trees** **dri**ving a **lorry**
 practising **foot**ball **dra**wing a **line**

Unit 26

silent r

girl

> The letter r is silent in all the words in this unit.
> r is pronounced only in front of a vowel.

Exercise 1

Listen and repeat:

a **horse**   a **bird**   a **girl**   a **church**

Make sentences with these words: **large**, **short**, **warm**, **thir**sty

EXAMPLE:

That's a **large church**.

Listen and repeat:

a **fork**   a **gar**den   a **card**

a **farm**

a **car**pet

a **mar**ket

Make sentences with these words: **large, dir**ty

EXAMPLE:

What a **large fork**!

Exercise 2

Reading

THE WORST STUDENT

Irma

It's | **Saturday mor**ning |
   | **Thurs**day after**noon** |

Irma is **lear**ning **Eng**lish and she's **wor**king **hard**. She's **lear**ning **thir**ty **words. Ir**ma **does**n't under**stand** the **first word.** She's the **worst stu**dent in the **world**.

Do you understand these thirteen words?

arm	**thir**ty	e**x**ercise	four**teen**	impor**tant**
dark	**for**ty	**yes**terday	for**get**	
hers	**par**ty			
worse				
north				

Sentence practice

EXAMPLES:

I **under**stand the **word** "**arm**".

I **don't** under**stand** the **word** "**north**".

Unit 27

r/silent r

her apples/her books

> Remember:
> The letter r is pronounced only in front of a vowel.

Exercise 1

Listen and repeat:

Mary

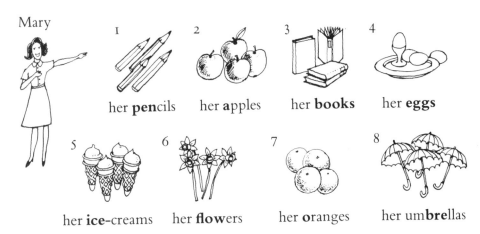

1 her **pen**cils   2 her apples   3 her **books**   4 her **eggs**

5 her **ice**-creams   6 her **flow**ers   7 her **or**anges   8 her um**brel**las

Sentence practice

EXAMPLES:

They're her pencils.
She's got four pencils.
They're your pencils, Mary.

Exercise 2

Make sentences from this table:

1	2	3	4	5
That's	her your our their	angry English funny clever interesting old new	teacher	over **there** near the **door** in the **corner** at the **window** under the **light** next to the **blackboard** behind the table in **front** of the **blackboard**

EXAMPLE:

That's our **clever tea**cher **over there**.

Unit 28

ɪə

beer

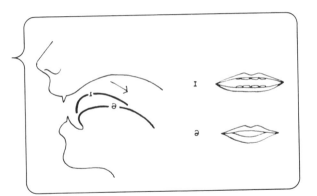

eə

chair

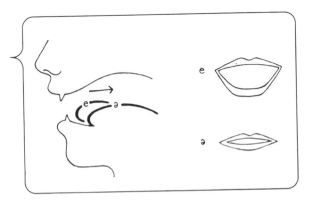

Exercise 1

Listen and repeat:

sound 1	sound 2
near	where
here	there

Excuse me. Where's the ⋆**air**port? Is it **near here**?

Yes. It's **there.**

⋆Substitute: **ae**roplane
hairdresser's
square

72

Exercise 2

Sentence practice

EXAMPLE:

Student A: There's a **news**paper on the table.

Student B: **Yes.** But **my news**paper **isn't** │**there**│.
│**here**│

Exercise 3

Dialogue:

A: **Where's** my ⋆**pen**?

B: I **don't know.** There's a **pen** on the table.

A: **Yes.** But **my pen isn't** │**there**│.
│**here**│

B: │**There**│it is! It's on the **chair**.
│**Here**│

⋆Substitute words from the picture.

Unit 29

ʊ

book

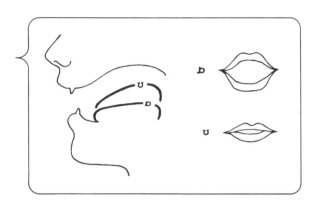

Exercise 1

Listen and repeat:

	sound 1	sound 2	
	cock	cook	
	lock	look	
	box	books	

Look at the pairs of sentences below. Put a tick against the sentences you hear.
a) What a noisy cock!   What a noisy cook!
b) I want a lock.   I want a look.
c) Give me the box, please. Give me the books, please.

74

Exercise 2

Listen and repeat:

a cook

cookery books

The cooking pot is full

a box of wood

SUGAR

Water is falling on the cook's foot

Exercise 3

Sentence practice

EXAMPLES:

a)

Look! He's **pu**shing it. **Don't push** it! **Pull** it!

b)

Look! He's **pu**lling it. **Don't pull** it! **Push** it!

I

2

PULL

3

4

5

6

Unit 30

u:

boot

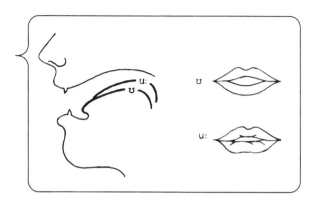

Exercise 1

Listen and repeat:

	sound 1	sound 2	
	look	Luke	
	pull	pool	

Look at the pairs of sentences below. Put a tick against the sentences you hear.

a) Here's the pen. Look! It's on the table.　Here's the pen. Luke! It's on the table.

b) It says "PULL" on this door.　It says "POOL" on this door.

77

Exercise 2 🔲

Dialogue:

June: Do you **like** ★mu̇sic?

Sue: **Yes,** I d̂o.

June: **I** like **mu**sic **t̂oo**.

★Substitute:
A	B	C
cooking	**Luke**	**good food**
football	**fruit**	**blue rooms**
good books	**this school**	**good schools**
this room	**blue shoes**	**look**ing at **pools**
lots of **su**gar	**swi**mming **pools**	**look**ing at the **moon**

Unit 31

t

tin

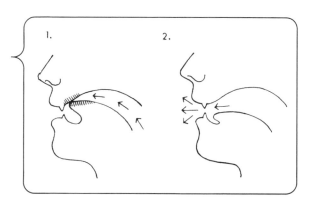

1.

2.

Exercise 1

Listen and repeat:

a **te**lephone   a **te**levision   a **tea**cup   a **ta**ble

Sentence practice

EXAMPLES:

What a **pre**tty **te**lephone!
What a **dir**ty **te**levision!

a **le**tter   a **tea**spoon   a **toy**

Exercise 2

Listen and repeat:

I   a **fat cat**   **fat cats**

79

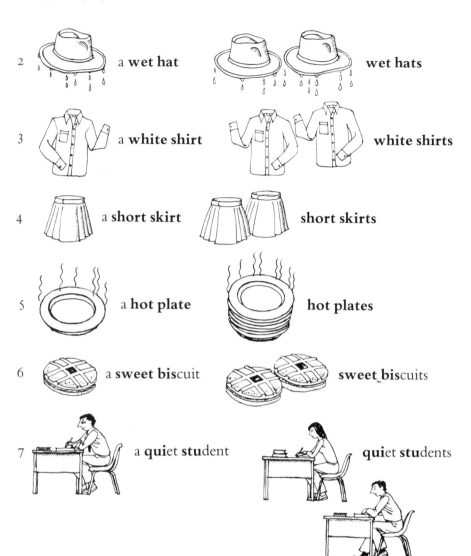

2   a **wet hat**   **wet hats**

3   a **white shirt**   **white shirts**

4   a **short skirt**   **short skirts**

5   a **hot plate**   **hot plates**

6   a **sweet bis**cuit   **sweet_bis**cuits

7   a **quiet stu**dent   **quiet stu**dents

Sentence practice

EXAMPLE: Picture 1

Student A: **What's that?**   Student B: | That's | a **cat**.
                                         | It's |

Student A: **What a fat cat!**   Student B: **What fat cats!**

80

Unit 32

d

door

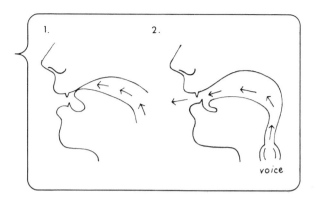

1. 2.

voice

Exercise 1

Listen and repeat:

	sound 1	sound 2	
	Ted	dead	
	write	ride	
	cart	card	

Look at the pairs of sentences below. Put a tick against the sentences you hear.

a) Look! It's Ted.　　　Look! It's dead.
b) He can write well.　He can ride well.
c) That's a nice cart.　That's a nice card.

81

Exercise 2

Listen and repeat: sad   hard   wide   old   cold   round

Choose the right word:

1   2    3

a .... bed   a .... bird   a .... head

4   5

   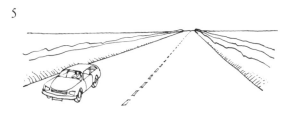

an .... friend   a .... road

6

a .... wind

Sentence practice

EXAMPLE: Picture 1

Student A: Do you **like hard beds**?

Student B: | **Yes, I do**
            | **No, I don't** |. Do **you**?

Student A: | **Yes, I do**
            | **No, I don't** |.

82

Exercise 3

Choose the right word: red   bad   good   wide   old   cold

1

a .... dog

2

a .... day

3

a .... desk

4

a .... doctor

5

an .... door

6

a .... dress

Unit 33

aʊ

house

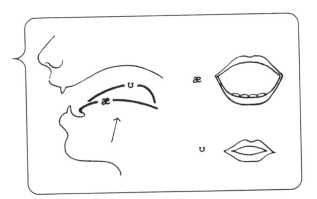

Exercise 1

Listen and repeat:

	sound 1	sound 2

car   cow

can't   count

Look at the pairs of sentences below. Put a tick against the sentences you hear.

a) He's got a new car.　　He's got a new cow.

b) These children can't.　These children count.

84

Exercise 2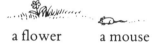

Listen and repeat:

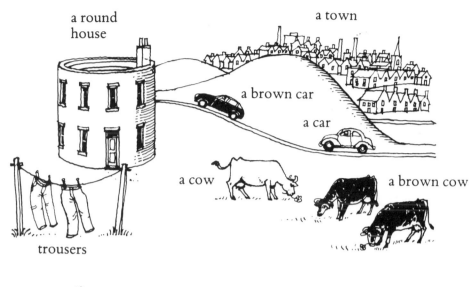

a round
house

a town

a brown car

a car

a cow

a brown cow

trousers

a flower   a mouse

There are a **thou**sand **hou**ses in the **town**.
Count the cows in the picture.

Sentence practice

EXAMPLE:

Student A: **How** many ⋆**cows** are there?

Student B: There are **three cows**.

⋆Substitute:

cars	**flow**ers	**brown cows**
towns	**hou**ses	**round hou**ses
mice	**brown cars**	**pairs** of **trou**sers

Unit 34

əʊ

phone

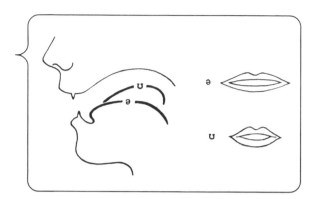

Exercise 1

Listen and repeat:

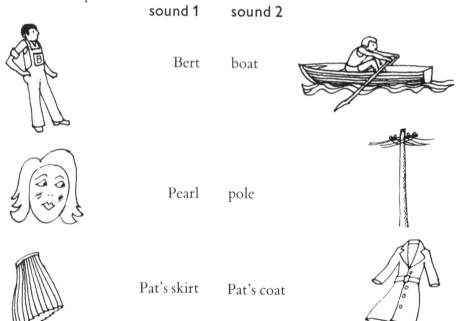

	sound 1	sound 2	
	Bert	boat	
	Pearl	pole	
	Pat's skirt	Pat's coat	

Look at the pairs of sentences below. Put a tick against the sentences you hear.

a) That's my Bert.   That's my boat.
b) There are two Pearls here.   There are two poles here.
c) Pat's skirt is very pretty.   Pat's coat is very pretty.

Listen and repeat:

 sound 1   sound 2

   saw   sew   

   hall   hole   

   all doctors   old doctors

Look at the pairs of sentences below. Put a tick against the sentences you hear.

a) Do you like sawing?   Do you like sewing?

b) There's a big hall at the front of the house.   There's a big hole at the front of the house.

c) I like all doctors.   I like old doctors.

Exercise 2 .

Listen and repeat:

Hello!

Hello!

a warm coat

a cold nose

no coat

cold toes

Joan's dog

It's a cold morning.
It's snowing.
Joan is going for a walk with her dog.

Dialogue:

A: He**llo**!
B: He**llo**!
A: **Where** are you **go**ing? **Are** you going **home**?
B: **No**. I'm **go**ing to ★.......................
A: **Oh**!
B: **Where** are **you** going? Are **you** going **home**?
A: **No**. **I'm** going to ★.......................

★Substitute:
Paul's house   the ho**tel**   the **shop** round the **cor**ner
Dr. **Jones**'s house   the **green**grocer's   the **tele**phone down the **road**
the **gro**cer's   the **post** office

Unit 35

s/linking s

Exercise 1

Listen and repeat:

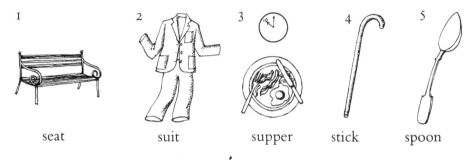

1	2	3	4	5
seat	suit	supper	stick	spoon

6	7	8
street	stamp	slipper

s   this   it's
this seat   this suit   this skirt   this spoon

whose seat   whose supper   his seat   Sam's supper

Sentence practice

EXAMPLE: Picture 1

Student A: Do you like this seat?

Student B: Yes. It's a nice seat.

Student A: Whose seat is it?

Student B: It's | Sam's seat.
          | his seat.

Exercise 2

1

Luke

2

Janet

3

Pat

4

Paul

5

Ted

6

Sue

EXAMPLE:

Student A: Who's ꙸ*sewing?

Student B: Janet's sewing.

*Substitute:
smiling	sitting down	speaking to Mary
sleeping	saying hello	standing at the bus stop
swimming	speaking to Pat	
studying	stopping a bus	

Unit 36

∫

shoe

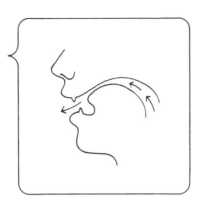

Exercise 1

Listen and repeat:

	sound 1	sound 2	
	sea	she	
	Sue	shoe	
	puss	push	

Look at the pairs of sentences below. Put a tick against the sentences you hear.

a) Sea's very quiet today.   She's very quiet today.
b) There are two Sues here.   There are two shoes here.
c) Come here! Puss!   Come here! Push!

Exercise 2

Listen and repeat:

1

Scottish
English

2

British
Irish

3

Danish
Swedish

4

French
Spanish

5

Finnish
Russian

6

Polish
Turkish

Sentence practice

EXAMPLES: Picture 1

1 Student A: Is she **Sco**ttish?

   Student B: **No**, she **is**n't. She's **En**glish.

2 Student A: Is she **Sco**ttish or **En**glish?

   Student B: She's **En**glish.

Unit 37

3

television

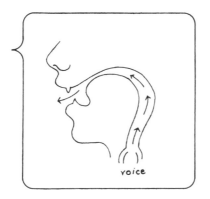

Exercise 1

What does **Sue us**ually do?
Monday ✓
Tuesday ✓
Wednesday ✓
Thursday ✓
Friday ✓
Saturday ×
Sunday ×

1   wakes **up**

2   gets **up**

3   has **break**fast

4   leaves **home**

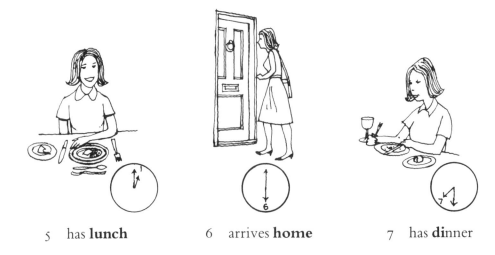

5 has **lunch**   6 arrives **home**   7 has **dinner**

8 goes to **bed**

Sue usually wakes **up** at **se**ven o'**clock**.
Now ask and answer questions about Sue.

EXAMPLE:

Student A: **What time** | does she **us**ually wake **up**?
            When

Student B: She **us**ually wakes **up** at **se**ven o'**clock**.

Unit 38

tʃ

cherry

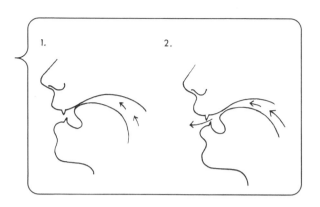

Exercise 1

Listen and repeat:

	sound 1	sound 2	
	sherry	cherry	
	sheep	cheap	
	wash	watch	

Look at the pairs of sentences below. Put a tick against the sentences you hear.

a) Which is the best sherry?   Which is the best cherry?
b) That's a sheep farm.   That's a cheap farm.
c) She's washing the television.   She's watching the television.

Exercise 2

Listen and repeat:

the **kit**chen

a chair

cheese

chocolate
cake

a **pic**ture of some **child**ren

chicken

fish and **chips**

a watch

CHERRY

CHINESE FOOD

SUGAR

the **kit**chen **table**

cherry pie

chalk

a match

Sentence practice

Make sentences beginning:
A. There's a ....

B. There's some ....

EXAMPLES:

A. There's a chair behind the
   kitchen table.

B. There's some cheese on the
   kitchen table.

Exercise 3

Look at the picture again. Now ask and answer questions.

EXAMPLE:

Student A: **How** much ⋆**cheese** is there?

Student B: There's | **enough**
                    | **too** much | **cheese** for † **two child**ren's **lunch**.
                    | **too** little

Substitute: ⋆examples from the picture in Exercise 2 †other numbers

96

Unit 39

dʒ
jam

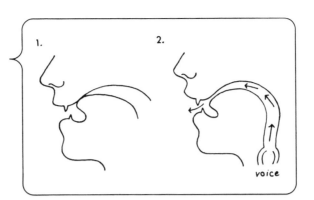

Exercise 1

Listen and repeat:

	sound 1	sound 2	
	cherry	Jerry	
	cheap	jeep	
	choke	joke	

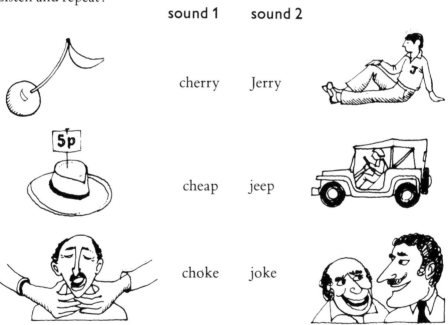

Look at the pairs of sentences below. Put a tick against the sentences you hear.

a) Is your name Cherry?   Is your name Jerry?
b) I want a cheap type of car.   I want a jeep type of car.
c) I'm choking.   I'm joking.

97

Exercise 2

Listen and repeat:

What's in the **large fridge**?   **What's** in the **small fridge**?

chicken   **Ger**man **sau**sage

cabbage   cheese

vegetables   oranges

jelly   a **jar** of **jam**

cherry **pie**   **choc**olate **cake**

Now ask and answer questions.

Which fridge is the cheese in?

The large fridge.

EXAMPLE:

Student A: **Which fridge** is the **je**lly in?

Student B: The **small** fridge.

Exercise 3 🔲

Reading

A **new sho**pping centre has **three bu**tcher's shops **next** to each other.
The **name** of **each bu**tcher is **Joe**.
When the **three bu**tcher's shops **o**pen, the **first bu**tcher **writes a**bove
his **shop**: '**Joe's** – the **Lar**gest **B**utcher's **Shop**'.
The **se**cond **butcher writes a**bove his **shop**: '**Joe's** – the **Chea**pest
Butcher's **Shop**'.
The **third bu**tcher **writes above his shop** in **large le**tters: '**JOE'S**
BUTCHER'S SHOP – **MAIN EN**TRANCE'.

Unit 40

j

yellow

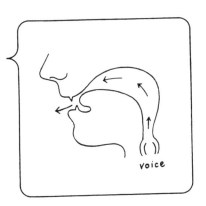

Exercise 1

Listen and repeat:

you	**new**	**thank** you
yes	**mu**sic	Portu**guese**
year	**Jan**uary	**Ha**ppy New **Year**!
yellow	**stu**dent	

Exercise 2

At a New Year Party

Happy New **Year**!

Thank you. **Ha**ppy New **Year** to **you too**!

Do you **like** this **new mu**sic?

Yes, I **do**.

This is **John**.
He's a **student**.

How do you **do**?

I **like** your
glasses.

Thank you.
They're **new**.

Do you **speak** Portu**guese**?

Yes, I **do**.

Do you **like** this
orange **j**elly?

Yes. But the
yellow **j**elly's
better!

Jim likes **telling j**okes,
doesn't he?

Yes, he **does**.

Which question do you
always **an**swer "**Yes**" to?

How do you
pro**nounce**
Y – E – S?

Unit 41

eɪ

tail

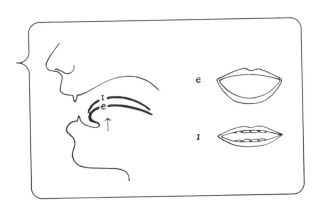

Exercise 1

Listen and repeat:

	sound 1	sound 2	
	pepper	paper	
	sell	sail	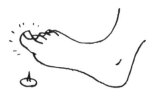
	pen	pain	

Look at the pairs of sentences below. Put a tick against the sentences you hear.

a) Pass me the pepper, please.   Pass me the paper, please.

b) He's selling his boat.   He's sailing his boat.

c) I've got a bad pen.   I've got a bad pain.

Exercise 2

Listen and repeat:

Mrs Grey · plates · rain · the date · a radio · an aeroplane · James · Fay · a station · a table · a newspaper · a train · a gate · a railway · a baby

It's **rai**ning to**day**.
Mrs **Grey** is **ma**king a **cake**.
James and **Fay** are **play**ing a **game**.

Answer these questions:

EXAMPLE:

Student A: **What's** Mrs **Grey ma**king?
Student B: A **cake**.

1 **What's James play**ing with?
2 **What's Fay play**ing with?
3 **What's** the **ba**by **play**ing with?
4 **What's** the **date** to**day**?
5 **Spell** the **ba**by's **name**.
6 **Is** the **ba**by **play**ing with **pe**pper?

Unit 42

ɔɪ

boy

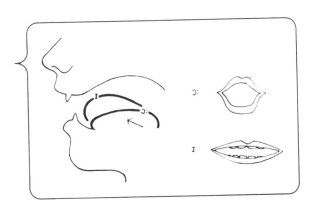

Exercise

Listen and repeat:

a noise

a boy

a toy

These are **noi**sy **boys**.
These are **noi**sy **toys**.

Make sentences about the toys in Unit 41 Exercise 2.

EXAMPLE:

It's a **toy train**.

104

Unit 43

aɪ

fine

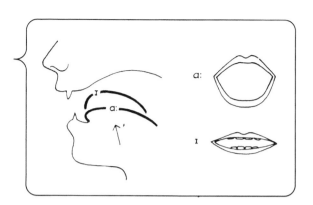

Exercise 1

Listen and repeat:

	sound 1	sound 2	
	R	I	
	Pa	pie	
	cart	kite	

Look at the pairs of sentences below. Put a tick against the sentences you hear.

a) His name's R. Smith. His name's I. Smith.
b) Here's an apple, Pa. Here's an apple pie.
c) That boy has a cart. That boy has a kite.

Exercise 2

Listen and repeat:

a)

wine

wide ties

sunshine

driving

climbing

riding

saying Good**bye**

this exercise

b)

rice

white mice

bright lights

ice-cream

writing

ice-skating

kite flying

saying Good**night**

Sentence practice

EXAMPLES:

I **like dri**ving.
I **don't** like **rice**.

Exercise 3

Dialogue:

A: **What** are you **do**ing on **Fri**day?

B: I'm **go**ing ***cli**mbing.

A: **Have** a **nice time**!

B: **Thanks**. **Bye**!

A: **Bye**!

*Substitute:

riding	**horse**-riding
cycling	**ice**-skating
driving	**kite**-flying

Unit 44

p

pen

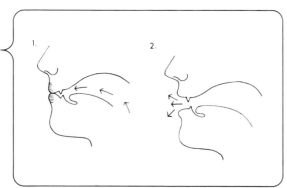

b

baby

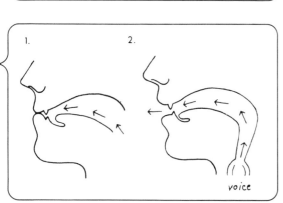

voice

Exercise 1

Listen and repeat:

	sound 1	sound 2
	pin	bin
	pen	Ben
	pear	bear

Look at the pairs of sentences below. Put a tick against the sentences you hear.

a) Have you got a pin?   Have you got a bin?
b) That's my pen.   That's my Ben.
c) There's a pear in the garden.   There's a bear in the garden.

Exercise 2

Listen and repeat:

a)

| a **pic**ture | a **pa**per plate | a **pink** pencil | some potatoes | a **pe**pper pot |

b)

a **cup**   an **en**velope   a **stamp**   a **pipe**   a **sheep**

c)

a **book**   a **bag**   a **big ball**   some **bread** and **bu**tter

a **bo**ttle of **beer**

Exercise 3

Listen and repeat:

	sound 1	sound 2	
	cap	cab	
	cup	cub	
	pup	pub	

Look at the pairs of sentences below. Put a tick against the sentences you hear.

a) I want a cap.   I want a cab.
b) That's a nice little cup.   That's a nice little cub.
c) What a noisy pup!   What a noisy pub!

Exercise 4

Listen and repeat:

butcher   **foot**baller   He's a **bar**man in a **pub**.
baker   **bus** driver   He's a **bar**man in a **club**.
builder   **cab** driver
barman

Sentence practice

EXAMPLE: Picture 1

Student A: **What's** his **job**?

Student B: He's a **buil**der.

Exercise 5

Game: Bob Went to Paris

Use the pictures in Exercises 1, 2 and 3.

EXAMPLE:

Student A: **Bob** went to **Pa**ris and he **bought** a **pipe**.

Student B: **Bob** went to **Pa**ris and he **bought** a **pipe** and a **bag**.

Student C: **Bob** went to **Pa**ris and he **bought** a **pipe**, a **bag** and a **cab**.

Unit 45

k

key

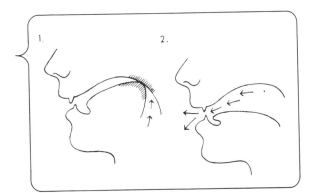

g

girl

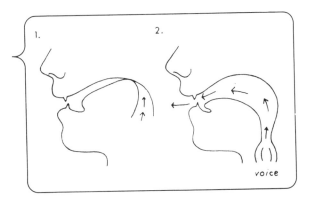

Exercise 1 🔲

Listen and repeat:

sound 1	sound 2
class	glass
coat	goat

curl   girl

Look at the pairs of sentences below. Put a tick against the sentences you hear.

a) That's a very small class.   That's a very small glass.
b) I've got a white coat.   I've got a white goat.
c) What a pretty little curl!   What a pretty little girl!

Exercise 2

Listen and repeat:

Be careful!   **Be qui**et!   **Be quick**!

    count   **Count** the **cups**. **Be quick**!

cake   **Cut** the **cake**. **Be care**ful!

   **clean**   **Clean** the **kit**chen. **Be qui**et!

   breakfast   **Cook** the **break**fast. **Be qui**et!

coffee   **Make** the **coffee**. **Be quick**!

cups   **Carry** the **cups**. **Be care**ful!

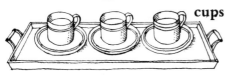

113

Sentence practice

EXAMPLE:

Student A: **Carry the cûps. Be cãreful!**

Student B: **Carry the cups cãrefully.**

Exercise 3

Listen and repeat:

	sound 1	sound 2	
	back	bag	
	clock	clog	
	Dick	dig	

Look at the pairs of sentences below. Put a tick against the sentences you hear.

a) There's something on your back.

   There's something on your bag.

b) That shop sells clocks.

   That shop sells clogs.

c) That boy Dick's in the garden.

   That boy digs in the garden.

Exercise 4

Listen and repeat:

dog   egg   leg   fig   frog

dogs   eggs   cakes

figs   books   frogs

clocks

Sentence practice

EXAMPLE:

Mr **Green** likes **dogs**.

Unit 46

S   sun

Z   zoo

Exercise 1

Monday ✓
Tuesday ✓
Wednesday ✓
Thursday ✓
Friday ✓

1

2

3

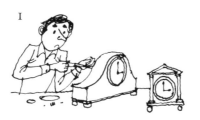

4

5

6

7

8

9

10

36 ... 37 ....
38 ... 39 ....
40 ... 41 ....

11

12

Ha Ha!

Ha Ha
Ha Ha

Listen and repeat:

writes books	stops trucks	asks questions
makes clocks	eats chips	visits friends
breaks plates	cooks breakfasts	tells jokes
cuts cakes	helps students	counts heads

Sentence practice

EXAMPLE:

Student A: **Which man writes books**?

Student B: The **third** man **writes books**.

Exercise 2

Listen and repeat:
Mr   Mrs   Miss   Ms

1 Mrs Long

2 Mrs Jones

3 Miss Smith

How do you spell it?

4 Mr Monday

5 Ms Love

6 Miss Young

7 Mrs Grey

8 Mr Black

9 Mrs Monday

10 Mr Wilson

11 Ms James

12 Mr Green

Listen and repeat:

cleans walls	spells words	washes clothes
digs holes	rides bicycles	sells watches
sings songs	rings bells	teaches horses
telephones friends	loves dogs	watches football matches

Sentence practice

EXAMPLE:

Student A: **Who cleans wȃlls?**

Student B: Mrs **Lȏng** cleans **walls.**

Answers to recorded recognition exercises

Unit 2
a) Look at that zoo!
b) Listen to that bus!
c) Ten pence, please.

Unit 4
a) Is that a mouse?
b) Look at this sum.
c) It's thick.

Unit 7
a) Look at the ship.
b) These are beans.
c) Is this a mill?

Unit 10
a) He's a vet student.
b) There's a little wine here.
c) That's a veil.

Unit 13
a) These are nice.
b) That's my little Tim.
c) That's her money.

Unit 14
a) Please don't sing!
b) Are you sinking?

Unit 15
a) Have you got a pin?
b) That's my Ben.
c) That tin is very small.

Unit 16
a) Her name is Miss N. Smith.
b) That's a very big X.
c) Have you got a pan?

Unit 17
a) Is this your cup?
b) Look at that little hut.
c) That's a very bad cat.

Unit 18
Part A
a) I've got a little cat.
b) That's a lovely heart.

Part B
a) That's a very bad cart.
b) Look at that hut.

Unit 20
a) I want a white cot, please.
b) That pot is very strong.
c) There's a sack on the floor.

Unit 21
a) Is your name Don?
b) That's a very big pot.
c) We don't want the forks in here.

Unit 23
a) Is your name Pearl?
b) I want white shorts, please.
c) He walks in the garden.

Unit 24
Part A
a) It's a lovely night.
b) Draw a line.
c) He loves Jenny.

Part B
a) That's my bin.
b) He's in.
c) He wants a pill.

Unit 25
a) It's a long sum.
b) Mary likes Jerry.
c) There's a flower in the glass.

Unit 29
a) What a noisy cock!
b) I want a lock.
c) Give me the books, please.

Unit 30
a) Here's the pen. Look! It's on the table.
b) It says "Pool" on this door.

Unit 32
a) Look! It's Ted.
b) He can write well.
c) That's a nice cart.

Unit 33
a) He's got a new car.
b) These children count.

Unit 34
Part A
a) That's my boat.
b) There are two poles here.
c) Pat's skirt is very pretty.

Part B
a) Do you like sewing?
b) There's a big hall at the front of the house.
c) I like all doctors.

Unit 36
a) She's very quiet today.
b) There are two shoes here.
c) Come here! Puss!

Unit 38
a) Which is the best sherry?
b) That's a cheap farm.
c) She's washing the television.

Unit 39
a) Is your name Jerry?
b) I want a cheap type of car.
c) I'm choking.

Unit 41
a) Pass me the pepper, please.
b) He's selling his boat.
c) I've got a bad pain.

Unit 43
a) His name's R. Smith.
b) Here's an apple pie.
c) That boy has a cart.

Unit 44
Part A
a) Have you got a bin?
b) That's my pen.
c) There's a pear in the garden.

Part B
a) I want a cab.
b) That's a nice little cup.
c) What a noisy pup!

Unit 45
Part A
a) That's a very small glass.
b) I've got a white goat.
c) What a pretty little girl!

Part B
a) There's something on your bag.
b) That shop sells clogs.
c) That boy Dick's in the garden.